# BANKRUPTCY SECRETS LIVE! FROM THE LAS VEGAS STRIP

By
## Ryan Really/Ruehle
Attorney—Teacher—Veteran

RYAN J. RUEHLE
ATTORNEY AT LAW, LLC

Ryan Ruehle
*Admitted in Ohio-Kentucky-Florida*
www.BankruptcyLawyerInCincinnati.com
www.GetReallyLegal.com
info@GetReallyLegal.com
(513) 621-0999
Fax: (513) 445-5833

**A FRIEND OF THE FAMILY ™**

**Bankruptcy Secrets LIVE! from the Las Vegas Strip**
Copyright 2016 by Ryan Ruehle. All Rights Reserved.
Published by Really Media.

ISBN-13: 978-0692805596
ISBN-10: 0692805591

# DEDICATION

To my wife Chrissann, and my family and friends for their support over the years.

To my past supervisors, co-workers, professors, teachers, and classmates for helping me make sense of this exciting journey called life.

I want to thank God and thank you for purchasing this book.

# CONTENTS

# INTRODUCTION

## The Name Game

My given last name is spelled Ruehle which is correctly pronounced "really" and it has been mispronounced all my life. As for the Las Vegas-themed book title, I was staying at the legendary and now demolished Riviera Hotel and Casino in Las Vegas on business and pleasure. We had two days of video interviews scheduled at two different locations. I was interviewing Dr. Kenneth Manges for a new bankruptcy video series I was producing on the psychological effects of bankruptcy (which is posted on YouTube). After the interview, we moved from a downtown "Old Vegas" law office location I rented for the shoot to the 808 Post & Production Studios just off the Strip.

I prefer being behind the scenes, behind the camera or interviewing but it wasn't long before my producer and friend Mark Ott at 808 Production Studios had parked me in front of the camera as well. We decided that we would start shooting my answers to Bankruptcy's Most Frequently Asked Questions on video.

This book is what my clients ask about before they

hire me and this is what in confidence I tell them. There is nothing like having a quiet conversation.

# A Quiet Conversation

What do I mean by this? If a friend or a friend's friend approached me at a Saturday afternoon barbeque with a glass of sweet tea or Ale 8 and started asking me questions about bankruptcy, I would provide them the following responses in plain English. No coats and ties, no conference room tables, simply talking by ourselves under a shade tree or 10' x 10' pop-up canopy with backyard noises in the background.

I don't talk to people or potential clients like I speak in the courtroom or when I am teaching a college course or legal seminar unless that is what they want; legalese, terms of art, case law, etc. While I do provide bankruptcy advice to other attorneys on a daily basis, and we professionally discuss the nuances of law and procedures, this book was not written as a practice manual or treatise for the bar or my attorney friends. They don't need a book as they already have saved my cell phone number in their contacts.

# CONFIDENTIAL ANSWERS TO CONSUMER BANKRUPTCY'S FREQUENTLY ASKED QUESTIONS

There are two types of bankruptcies that we normally file in our office: Chapter 7 and Chapter 13. A Chapter 7 takes about four months to complete. Some people call it a straight bankruptcy. The purpose of Chapter 7 is to see if you own anything that has any equity in it and is considered to be non-exempt which means it cannot be protected by the laws that allow you to keep the shirt off your back. Here is an extreme example:

> You have a closet filled with nothing but Versace clothing and file for Chapter 7. While the Court doesn't want to take the everyday shirt off your back, rest assured they may be interested to see if they can take that entire collection of items, sell them, turn them into cash and pay a little something back to your creditors. Even if they only receive only ten percent of what you owe them; that is actually a good day for your creditors in a Chapter 7. In return you walk away from your debts.

That is a crazy example! Generally, the court is looking for large tax refunds, money in the bank, real estate and late model vehicles with equity. But anything you own will be reviewed and your attorney can show you how to protect it before you file. In rare circumstances, if you still have a lot of unnecessary or luxury goods/vehicles that you have not sold prior to bankruptcy you may have to surrender them to the court so they can sell them, turn them into cash and pay a little something back to your creditors. But most people have voluntarily returned or sold these items before they come in hoping to avoid bankruptcy.

Chapter 13, on the other hand, allows you to pay back something to your creditors over a three to five year period. Chapter 13 gives you options. Chapter 13 is good for people who are behind on a home they want to keep. We can cure the past due amount on the mortgage. We can also stop crazy interest and penalties on most tax debts. We can pay some of those tax debts in full, and at the end of the day, the unsecured creditors, such as credit cards, medical bills and the like, will end up getting whatever is left over; maybe paying one to five cents on the dollar. There are a lot of reorganizing options with a Chapter 13 like getting rid of the rental property that will not sell and the debt while keeping your home, reducing interest rates on bad car loans, etc. Attorneys can help you pick and choose and create a Chapter 13 plan and payback for your family's financial situation.

Chapter 13 is a three to five year blanket approach to your money problems. Chapter 7 is a straight bankruptcy that provides freedom and takes only four months to complete. You get in and out of court a little more quickly, but you may have to give up some assets.

## What are the Advantages of Chapter 7 Bankruptcy Over Chapter 13?

The advantages of Chapter 7 bankruptcy over Chapter 13 include that you normally don't have to pay anything back to your creditors. You get to hold on to most, if not all, of your items because you don't have a bunch of luxury goods or items that are paid off. Most Chapter 7 cases are called No-Asset Cases and you keep everything. That's not true in every case, but in most cases, it's the way it works.

Also in Chapter 7, it only takes you four months to complete and I value the freedom that Chapter 7 gives people. In approximately three and a half to four months after we file your case and go to one hearing, you're done. You have your fresh start. It's a new chapter in life and you can get on with it.

# What are the Advantages of Chapter 13 Bankruptcy Over Chapter 7?

There are many reasons to choose Chapter 13 over Chapter 7. It can be a blanket approach that resolves one or a combination of problems

If you are behind on a house that you want to keep, you really need to consider Chapter 13 bankruptcy because we are going to catch up on your house using the Chapter 13 bankruptcy plan and prevent that mortgage company from filing or continuing to file a foreclosure on your home. If you love your home and you want to keep it and you're behind on it, we need to look at a Chapter 13 bankruptcy.

If you are behind on student loans and they are in default status, garnishing your paycheck, etc., Chapter 13 can stop the collections from Navient and the like.

If you are behind on car payments, and/or you signed a high interest car loan that is worth less than what you owe on it, Chapter 13 can modify your car loan with a lower interest rate and maybe a lower payment.

If you are behind on taxes or other government debt, we want to stop the penalties and interest, you need to look at Chapter 13 bankruptcy as an option. Again, we are going to take three to five years to pay that back without interest and penalties in most cases.

Finally, if you make above average income, you might not qualify for Chapter 7 and may be required to file Chapter 13. Why? Because the court believes that you have the ability to pay something back to your creditors. We can take advantage of a bad situation. If you make an appointment, we'll discuss those options in detail.

## Can I Keep My Car in Chapter 7?

Most people want to know whether or not they can keep their car in Chapter 7 bankruptcy. The answer is usually yes, and here's why. Most people don't have any equity in the car they are driving right now or their vehicle is worth so little that by the time they've paid off their car, the Court will not be interested in it.

For example, if you have a 2011 Chevrolet and you owe $19,000 on it and yet it's only worth $15,000, you have no equity, i.e. you are "under water". You cannot sell that vehicle and make any money on it, and in most cases neither can the court. If you are current on the vehicle, its insured, you want to keep it and the court is not interested in it, you are probably going to be able to go back to the bank and sign a Reaffirmation Agreement which will allow you to renew the loan and keep it. You also keep the payment.

# Can I Keep my Car If I File Chapter 13?

Most people get to keep their cars in Chapter 13 unless the payment is absolutely too high or you have more vehicles than is necessary. In fact, Chapter 13 is going to pay off the vehicles so that when you emerge out of Chapter 13, the vehicles will be paid off, the taxes will be cured if you have any past due taxes, and the house will be caught up if you were behind on your house to begin with. There are some options and benefits of Chapter 13 that are not available in Chapter 7. It's a good reorganization and you get to drive away into the sunset with your vehicle.

# Can I Keep My 401K?

Many people want to know whether or not the government can take their employee retirement accounts if they file bankruptcy. The answer is no if you truly have a retirement account that is protected as an ERISA based account. Some common examples are a 401(k), an IRA, a Roth IRA, and pensions. Those are all protected by the laws of bankruptcy and/or state law depending on your state. Essentially, unless you've made some recent transactions into those accounts that are questionable, the courts cannot touch your 401(k)s and IRAs in 99% of the cases. DON"T USE YOUR RETIREMENT TO PAY MEDICAL BILLS OR CREDIT CARDS!!! CALL US FIRST!!

# What If I Already Have a Lawsuit Against Me?

Unfortunately, if your creditor has already gotten a judgment against you, then you can look forward to wage garnishments, bank account garnishments and judgment liens against your property. Those are the three most common types of post-judgment collection activities. A bankruptcy can stop those activities and give you a breathing spell and probably eliminate those debts as well.

However, you don't want to wait until you're actually receiving a wage garnishment to contact an attorney. If you've been served with a Complaint, contact a bankruptcy attorney today. Generally, the longer you wait, the less options you will have available. It's going to be less expensive to head it off at the pass than wait until they've actually dug into your paycheck and home. Attorneys can help you out, but you have to give us time to do so.

# Can I File Chapter 7 Again?

Under the Bankruptcy Code, you can file a bankruptcy once every eight years. Of course, there are requirements as well that have to be done in good faith. Some people may have gone through the bankruptcy process once before, and maybe there's been a recent change in their life, whether it be reduced income, perhaps divorce, and if you have to file another bankruptcy, you can do so eight years after the date of your last bankruptcy filing.

Now, if it's been less than eight years and you still need bankruptcy relief, you can file a Chapter 13 bankruptcy. You do have some bankruptcy and non-bankruptcy options even though you filed before. Give us a call and we'll take a look at your situation to see if we can help you.

## How Does Bankruptcy Affect My Credit?

When you file Chapter 7, that bankruptcy information is going to stay on your credit report for up to ten years; Chapter 13 seven years. Now, most people believe that they are not going to be able to get credit for ten years. Well, that's just not true. This is America where you will be eligible for more credit opportunities as soon as you get your discharge. If fact, there are a lot of people who, once they file their bankruptcy, will start receiving offers from creditors for new car loans and gas cards before they attend their hearing! They usually have very high interest rates and are probably not your best option, but it is a good illustration that there is life after bankruptcy.

Generally, two years after your bankruptcy is when you might qualify for a home loan. During those 24 months, work on reestablishing good credit by getting a gas card or secured card and paying on time each and every month, including student loans. Use those crucial months to help you rebuild your credit so that you can get credit when you need it in the future. The credit industry standards change often, so do your own timely research on rebuilding your credit.

## If I File for Bankruptcy Do I Have to Give Up My Car? Will I Lose My Home?

There is a myth that most people will lose everything they own if they file a bankruptcy. Well, that's just not true. In fact, the opposite is true. Most people who file for Chapter 7 bankruptcy relief get to keep all of their items, household goods, cars and the like. The reason is that there are a number of exemptions under the law available to you. The exemption laws are different depending on each state but generally speaking, unless you have something in your home that's worth an extraordinary amount of money, you will likely keep all your everyday items.

They're not going to be interested in your living room furniture or your dog (that sleeps on that furniture), or your late model car that you still owe money on. All of those things are normally exempted from bankruptcy and a good bankruptcy attorney is going to be able to let you know before you file why you're going to get to keep those items, including your residence.

# What If Something Happens While I Am in a Chapter 13?

While you're in Chapter 13, if you're unable to make your payment, you do have some options available to you. Sometimes people can't make their payment because of a temporary job loss or sickness in the family or an emergency with the house. In those cases, the short term remedy is a Chapter 13 plan suspension. We suspend your plan payments for a couple months. That might require a plan modification later on down the road, but it does provide you with the relief you need to get back on track of this three to five year commitment.

# Do I Have to Include Everybody I Owe in My Bankruptcy?

Yes. The Bankruptcy Code requires you to list all the debts that you have. This includes your commercial debts that you might see on your credit report. It also includes people that you owe money to that aren't on your credit report. That can be a landlord or your brother-in-law. The Court requires you to list these people and the rationale is everyone gets treated fairly in the bankruptcy.

Some debtors don't list their favorite store's charge card, but they find out afterwards under normal circumstances, the accounts are going to be closed anyway. Because when you file your bankruptcy, the information is going to be electronically reported on the "grid", and the electronic notice will go out to your other creditors who are monitoring your credit report. I am told Wells Fargo checks the grid every 24 hours for their bank customers' bankruptcy filings. The creditors will go ahead and close those accounts to make sure that they're not liable for any more purchases.

## What If I Owe Child Support?

If you file a bankruptcy and you have a child support obligation of some kind, then you are required to let the Bankruptcy Court know this, even if you are current. You can expect the Bankruptcy Court, in either Chapter 7 or Chapter 13, to ask you about who is the recipient of the child support, usually the mother of the child, and you have to provide the court with an address. They are allowed to get notice of the bankruptcy just to insure that they get paid anything that might be owed to them. You may believe you are current with them, and that can be true, but you still have to list them and the Court still has to give them special notice.

# How are Court Fines and Government Overpayments Handled in Chapter 13 Bankruptcy?

Besides tax debts, there are other debts owed to governmental agencies such as traffic tickets, parking tickets, speeding tickets and criminal restitution. Perhaps you have some court costs that you owe the Clerk of Courts. Those debts are non-dischargeable in bankruptcy and they will have to be paid back. A lot of times if it's a parking ticket, the client may be advised to go ahead and pay those before the case is actually filed. On the other hand, if they cannot, then under normal circumstances, we are able to list those debts and they end up getting paid through the bankruptcy plan eventually. The preferred method is to take care of those smaller debts before you file your case, but that's not always possible. Keep that in mind if you are coming into Court to file bankruptcy that you do need to list those other types of governmental agency debts.

# How Do I Deal with Surviving Tax and Governmental Debts After Chapter 7 Bankruptcy?

If you owe the IRS or other state and local taxing entities, a Chapter 7 bankruptcy can give you the temporary relief by shedding the other types of debt you have so that after you complete your Chapter 7 in approximately 100 days, you can approach the IRS and come up with a repayment plan. We have found that most people can work with those governmental entities to come up with a repayment plan or offer in compromise after their bankruptcy is discharged. In extreme situations, filing a Chapter 13 after your Chapter 7 is an option for dealing with creditors who don't want to establish a payment plan you can manage.

## Should I Hire an Attorney?

People want to know whether or not they need an attorney for file bankruptcy and the short answer is absolutely. Not having an attorney in bankruptcy is a big mistake. You have too much to lose on the line if you have any type of property or if you have any type of income. You want it done right the first time, on time. There is nothing worse on a credit report than having a bankruptcy that was dismissed because you failed to complete the requirements. The court is generally not sympathetic to people who file bankruptcy by themselves, and in many cases, will hold you to the same standards as the attorneys are held to. If you are getting a tax refund exceeding $1,500.00 then it has been argued that you can use that money to afford a bankruptcy attorney.

Additionally, it is my opinion that the Bankruptcy Trustees do not like people filing their own cases.

They would never admit that. Bankruptcy questions at the hearing are confusing enough and can be tricky and pro-se filers are asked an additional series of questions about the preparation of these complex documents, who helped you prepare them, who did you pay to help you, etc., all under the penalty of perjury. Bottom line: Don't go it alone.

## The Bank is Foreclosing on My Home. Do I Need an Attorney?

When your home is foreclosed on, the bank is going to serve you a very thick set of papers that usually includes a copy of the Summons, the Complaint, and the documents you signed in order to purchase the home. That's going to include the Note and the Mortgage. When you get these documents, you need to see an attorney.

There are some non-bankruptcy options available as well as bankruptcy options. Our office, based on my experience, is able to do both. We can work with your creditors and may come up with terms that may allow you to stay in your home without filing bankruptcy. On the other hand, if we need to file bankruptcy, we'll go ahead and pull the trigger if we have to. Just know that in our office, you have options and we exercise those options.

# What is Loss Mitigation?

When you're foreclosed on and your house is at risk, the most frustrating thing is that the bank is likely going to start giving you what I call "double talk." Their attorneys, on one hand, are going to send you foreclosure papers, and at the same time their loss mitigation department is going to send you a hardship packet.

What you don't want to do is get confused by thinking that the loss mitigation department is working with the lawyers or the legal department to stop your bankruptcy! Nothing is further from the truth in most cases. The mortgage company is providing you with a few options, and if you are able to jump through their hoops and they are able to process your hardship package, then your foreclosure could be stopped.

However, the banks are not very good at loss mitigation. You need to come into the office and talk to an attorney once you receive your foreclosure papers, if not sooner. We'll be able to give you your options, whether it's bankruptcy or something else and help you save your home or strategically leave it.

The laws vary from state to state and each person's case may be different so consult with an attorney and do not take this as legal advice. In a majority of state courts, the creditor's job is to obtain a judgment against you for the full amount of the loan, and once they have that, then and only then, can a foreclosure sale be scheduled. The creditor has to advertise the foreclosure sale for a short period of time as to when the sale is going to take place, where it's going to take place and the minimum bid that is required in order to purchase the property. It's very dangerous to not have talked to a bankruptcy attorney before this date. If you wait until the last minute, you're probably going to have a hard time finding an attorney that is going to want to help. We do emergency filings and it is very expensive as there is a lot of work that has to be done, and it's not an easy process. Don't wait until the last minute.

## Can't We Just Shut the Utilities Off, Move Out, and Let the Bank Foreclose?

If your home in foreclosure is in a bad location, vandalized, mold damaged and/or there is otherwise something structurally wrong with your home then you may have some big problems. Just because the home has been foreclosed upon does not mean that the bank has to sell it. If they determine that the home will cost them more money than they will receive from the sale of the property, then they can cancel the sale or not schedule it at all and come after you for the balance of the foreclosure judgment.

These are extraordinary times right now, and we are

advising people in most circumstances to keep an eye on the property. Make sure that you don't just walk away and abandon it. There are some other dangers as well as the bank not being interested in selling the home. You could be responsible for taxes, homeowner's association fees, code violations for tall grass, etc. if a property hasn't been maintained. You need to keep an eye on your property. You don't want water pipes to freeze or the copper pipes and air conditioner stolen. Neighbors can help. Talk to a bankruptcy attorney or a foreclosure attorney so that you understand what strategies you need to protect your home.

## What About Divorce and Bankruptcy?

**Disclaimer: Entire Books are Written on Divorce and Bankruptcy, And It Cannot Be Completely Covered Here.**

A lot of times divorce and bankruptcy go hand in hand. Attorneys will often refer their clients to our office in order to file a bankruptcy as part of a divorce strategy. A primary reason is to eliminate a lot of property and debt settlement issues that would otherwise have to be tried in domestic relations court.

For example, if the individuals are not going to be able to hold onto the marital home based on one income, a very common scenario, then sometimes we file a Chapter 7 bankruptcy in order to allow one or both parties to discharge the debt. There are many bankruptcy issues with divorce, and your domestic relations attorney should be able to inform you about those issues if you approach them with bankruptcy on your mind.

## Can I File Bankruptcy on Child and Spousal Support?

In a divorce case, there are often child support and alimony issues as well as property settlement issues. And then surprise!-One party after the divorce goes ahead and files a bankruptcy.

What you have to understand is that those debts don't necessarily go away in Chapter 7 bankruptcy. You can still be held liable to your spouse for the debts that you agreed to take during the Separation Agreement or that were you were ordered to take by the Court. In Chapter 13, however, there are some options available to you and in Chapter 13 we start distinguishing between property settlements and maintenance, support and alimony payments. If it is in the nature of some type of property settlement and it qualifies under a number of legal tests, then those debts could be partially paid in Chapter 13 as general unsecured debts, perhaps paid ten cents on the dollar or five cents on the dollar or fifty cents on the dollar. Those debts are then discharged just like the credit cards and medical bills. For specific bankruptcy and divorce advice, consult a local attorney.

# Can a Bankruptcy Stop Water, Gas, and Electric Shutoffs?

If you're facing a shut-off notice or you have some high utility bills that have not been paid, those need to be listed on your bankruptcy. In Chapter 7, those debts do go away. However, in most states the utility company is entitled to ask you for a security deposit, which is normally equal to one month's usage. They can ask you for that up front in order to recommence service or sometimes they spread out the payments, but it does in most circumstances come back to you after 12 months in the form of a credit.

# Non-Bankruptcy Options

## Debt Consolidation

One of the first non-bankruptcy options I want to mention is **debt consolidation.** Under normal circumstances in debt consolidation a credit counseling agency might be able to help to avoid bankruptcy by combining most of your commercial debts in which you haven't been sued on yet. That would be things like credit cards, most commonly charge cards, those types of items. They usually have pre-set, negotiated rates with the credit card companies and you come up with one monthly payment. That monthly payment is made and they help provide over time a compromised debt settlement.

If you're going to look into one, I think you need to look to a local, non-profit credit counseling company who has normally pre-set negotiated terms with your credit cards. In most cases, they are able to provide you with some type of credit counseling along with a repayment plan. It's not for everybody, so if you're being sued, that's probably not going to resolve your issues. If you're being garnished, it's not going to resolve that either but if you approach your debt problem early enough, it might be a non-bankruptcy solution for you.

## Debt Settlement

Another option besides bankruptcy is **debt settlement**. Now, you have to be careful when you're dealing with debt settlement companies. Many have been sued and/or shut down by the government. Personally, I have not seen a lot of success stories with them. What happens with debt settlement is you send payments to some debt settlement company that is usually out of town, usually not affiliated with a law firm, and you've never met them. They don't have a local office and you've put a lot of faith and you've paid a lot of money. If you can find a local debt settlement company whose office you can visit and sit down and look them in the eye and make a determination of whether you'd like to hire them, then they may be potentially able to settle some debts for you. But, be careful.

What debt settlement companies usually promise is that they will settle your debts for pennies on the dollar. Most of them are out of town. Most clients have never met the debt settlement company and their staff and they've never talked to any attorney who is supposedly affiliated with those debt settlement companies. Nonetheless, they give them access to their bank account and send hundreds to thousands dollars a month. After a lot of time and money the debt settlement companies don't keep their promises-Surprise!

If you did find a honest one, in my opinion debt settlement companies have to bat a thousand. They have to settle each and every account. If you have one creditor who doesn't want to participate in the debt settlement plan and they sue you, you need to cancel that debt settlement plan and go seek some local legal help.

## How Do I Rebuild My Credit After Bankruptcy?

After you've received your bankruptcy discharge, you want to take some affirmative steps to help reestablish your credit. Some suggestions might be to go to www.annualcreditreport.com and take a look at your credit report and each of those accounts should be discharged. You want to start monitoring your credit and using things like secured credit cards. Oil company convenience store charge cards are popular and easy to get after bankruptcy. You want to continue to make payments on those debts that have survived your bankruptcy, perhaps a car payment that you wanted to keep making payments on. You need to be current each and every month on that. The same goes with student loans. If you do so, within 24 months after your bankruptcy, you're probably going to be looking at a lot better interest rates and that's what reestablishing your credit is, after all, all about, isn't it?

There is life after bankruptcy! If you know someone who has filed before you will likely see they survived and when it was all said and done, they were glad they did. After your bankruptcy is over with and you've received your bankruptcy discharge, you can rebuild your credit. Many clients obtain home ownership afterwards and you have gained your fresh start and financial freedom. Hopefully, you'll have some new wind in your sails and be able to use your debtor education materials to continue on and have a better financial future. When my clients call back a year or two later and I ask how they are doing with their fresh start, they all tell me that they are doing a lot better and thank you.

# What about Foreclosure Workouts/Loss Mitigation Options?

Foreclosure workouts have been around for as long as we've had mortgages in America. What happens is that if you are behind on your home, your mortgage company is going to notify their own loss mitigation department, and their job is to provide you with some workout options. Now, the reality is that they're not very good at these options. The banks are in business in order to make loans and profit from them. By compromising their loans, it undermines their business model. Nonetheless, they provide this service to individuals. Things that we need to talk about are loan modifications, short sales and deed in lieu of foreclosure.

If you are behind on your mortgage, the mortgage company is going to provide you information regarding a **loan modification**. They are going to ask you for a number of documents, ask you to prove your current income, to maybe write a message regarding any hardship that you are experiencing and they are going to take this information to see if you qualify for one of their loan modification programs. One "new" program (that may expire soon) is called the HAMP or Homeowners Affordability Modification Program. Despite all the promises that are made by the government, they're about as successful traditionally as the old loan modification programs. However, you are encouraged to apply for all loan modifications because if you are successful, you will help save your home without the need of filing a bankruptcy.

If you are behind on your home, your mortgage company may offer you a **forbearance agreement.** A forbearance traditionally allows you to make a lower monthly payment, usually it's the interest only payment, each and every months for about three to six months and then you'll be responsible for catching up on the past due amounts. They don't always work. They don't always solve the problem. But sometimes a forbearance can give you some temporary relief while you regroup and improve your income situation and repay your mortgage company.

If you are behind on your mortgage and you are able to catch up, you may have a contract right of **reinstatement.** You are supposed to request the "reinstatement figure" in writing (and most banks don't require the writing).  If you call the mortgage company they will usually send you a reinstatement letter within 7 days. This tells you the exact amount of lump-sum money they need to receive to get you current, usually certified funds by a date certain at a specific address. If they receive that money on that date, then you're officially caught up on your home. Now, good news-bad news! The good news is you are caught up. The bad news is that if a foreclosure has begun, that doesn't necessarily dismiss the foreclosure. The bank is going to hold your feet to the fire and stand on the sidelines waiting for you to make that next month's payment followed by the month after that's payment followed by the month after that's payment until you're back on track and they feel good about it or that the local judge has dismissed their case for not moving it.

---

## Chapter 13 is a Blanket Approach to Save your Home and Car as Well as Take Care of Student Loan, Credit Card, and Tax Issues

A **Chapter 13 bankruptcy** can save your home by giving you three to five years to catch up on your past due house payments. It can also take care of the real estate taxes that are owed and spread that out over a three to five year period so that if you owe $20,000.00 on your home in past due payments, you'll have three to five years to catch up on those payments.

When you file Chapter 13 bankruptcy, it's going to stay on your credit report for up to seven years. That will be reported against. That doesn't mean that you won't be able to get credit after seven years. It simply means that you may be subject to higher rates and you could be turned down by certain creditors. However, as I like to say, this is American and someone is going to offer you credit. You may not like the interest rate and you have to be aware of that but as long as there is an opportunity to obtain credit, someone is going to give you that opportunity.

## Short Sale

A lot of clients are looking for non-bankruptcy options to save their home, or perhaps a rental property they are no longer interested in. One of those options is a short sale. Like oil and water, if you're going to do a bankruptcy, you don't need to worry about a short sale in most cases. A short sale is where a written offer, usually provided by a realtor, is given to the bank and the bank either accepts or rejects the offer. It's usually an offered amount less than what you owe on the mortgage itself, so you're actually shorting the bank with the offer. Sometimes the banks will accept the offer. Sometimes they'll reject it. The problem is that meanwhile your foreclosure is continuing and while your house is in foreclosure and moving towards sheriff sale, a realtor has your house listed and they are trying to get the bank to accept it. Again, the banks aren't very good at these short sales and you risk the actual sale of the home and the deficiency balance that goes with it. Talk to an attorney before you consider a short sale.

## Deed in Lieu of Foreclosure

If you're not current on your home and the bank for some reason has not started a foreclosure lawsuit, one of your options is offering a deed in lieu of foreclosure. Instead of the bank incurring costs and fees in actually foreclosing on the home, you offer to sign the deed over to the bank. Sometimes the bank will do so on terms that allow you to walk away from the debt on the first mortgage where it's forgiven. Other times they'll ask you to sign a note that is unsecured for a certain sum.

## I Just Got Served a Foreclosure Complaint. Now What?

When the bank does foreclose upon your home, you're going to get the paperwork from their legal department and their attorneys informing you of the foreclosure. But, you're also going to hear from their loss mitigation department. Their job is to provide you options to save your home. The problem is they're not very good at it and the other problem is that the left hand doesn't know what the right hand is doing. So, a lot of clients make the mistake of putting all their faith in the loss mitigation department who is sending them information like a hardship package, talking about short sale options, talking about the HAMP, making homes affordable program, and it is in your best interest to fill out that paperwork. **Unfortunately, the banks aren't very good at processing the loan modifications.** Most banks are going to lose it. If they don't lose it, they're not going to give you an immediate answer, and in short, they're not going to process any options that are available fast enough before their right hand, the legal department, actually completes the foreclosure! You've got to manage both at the same time-the legal end of it and the loss mitigation end of it.

# Surrendering the House: Don't Walk Away. "You Have to Giftwrap the House to the Bank"

You can't just walk away from the house anymore because the banks are overwhelmed with housing inventory. You have to maintain and secure the place or have a trusted neighbor, relative or tenant do so.

For most, my advice is to stay in the house until after the foreclosure sale and thereafter until the DEED is out of your name and live rent free until they ask/make you move out. This usually takes months but can take years! Plus the mortgage company might actually pay you $800-$1600 to move out when its time.

If you cannot do that due to employment, etc. you are taking a risk on a huge asset. If you cannot stay in the home, you at least want to pay/trust a relative or neighbor to watch the house, mow the grass, keep the heroin addicts from taking the copper, etc.

Remember, the bankruptcy gets the LOAN out of your name but does not get the OWNERSHIP out of your name. If the house cabinets, bath fixtures, HVAC, are gone, the city has condemned it, squatters have set up residence, fire damage, etc. the bank can refuse to pay for a foreclosure and sale. This can rob you of your fresh start.

# APPENDIX A:
# OUR COMMITMENT TO ARMY VALUES

My military training and life experiences instilled strong character qualities including trustworthiness, caring, and compassion. And I bring those and other Army Values to work every day working with and for my clients. Can you apply these to your personal and professional life?

**Loyalty**
We are very loyal to our clients. We use all our knowledge, experience, and talents to bring about a successful outcome for clients. We've implemented the latest software systems and technology which enables us to effectively communicate with the courts and monitor the status of your case.

**Duty**
As a client, you can depend on us to follow through on their commitments and keep you apprised of the progress on your case.

**Respect**
We treat all our clients with the upmost respect and confidentiality. High levels of personal debt can be overwhelming and clients may sometimes feel disrespected by creditors. We understand that. We can help you regain the respect that you value and deserve.

## Selfless Service

At our law firm, providing high quality customer service is our number one priority. You will find we return calls and emails promptly. We want to make sure you have all the information and educational resources you need to be successful in your bankruptcy. We go the extra mile to help you get back on your feet and restore your families' financial health.

## Honor

Honor is a strong part of our work ethic at our firm. We always conduct ourselves in the most professional, trustworthy manner. We take pride in our work and we continuously seek the most effective bankruptcy solutions for our clients.

## Integrity

Integrity is a key part of our business. We will give you honest, straightforward advice about your case. In some cases, bankruptcy is not always the best solution. I will ask questions to fully understand your situation and discuss the best solutions for your specific case.

## Personal Courage

We are prepared to fight in the courtroom for you. We are well equipped with the knowledge, experience and resources to help you be successful in your bankruptcy, and meet your goals.

As you've heard, my military experience is an integral part of our firm's core values. We are prepared. Our firm is truly A Friend of the Family. Please call today to schedule a free consultation and we will lead your family down the path to financial freedom.

# APPENDIX B:
# HIRING OUR FIRM

Last year, there were over 789,222 non-business bankruptcies filed in the United States. As these statistics show, families are fighting for their financial freedom. Struggling with debt can be an extremely stressful and emotional experience. Our firm has stepped up and developed a strategy we call **Operation Debt Freedom**. Our motto is **Don't Fight Your Battle Alone.**

Our firm is **A Friend of the Family**. We have a successful track record in assisting individuals and their families with bankruptcy, foreclosure and other financial issues. Our firm focuses on bankruptcy solutions so we can provide the highest quality service and achieve the best possible outcomes for our clients. Our practice areas include Chapters 13 and 7 bankruptcies, foreclosure defense, and debt negotiation.

We have 3 easily accessible locations for your convenience. Our locations include: Downtown Cincinnati, West Chester, and Erlanger. We do offer evening and Saturday morning appointments as well.

You may be asking...Why Should I Contact Your Firm to Handle My Bankruptcy?

As our founding attorney, I have over 16 years of legal experience including serving 3 years as a Creditor Rights attorney for one of Kentucky's largest creditor rights' firms. I've developed an in-depth understanding of the processes, their language, and the strategies they use. As a result, I am able to anticipate their actions and I am a highly effective negotiator.

We regularly attend national seminars and conferences and seek new approaches and creative negotiation strategies for managing bankruptcies and debt resolutions. We implement those approaches to help our clients achieve better results.

I have over 30 years of military experience and I am a Veteran of Operation Iraqi Freedom. I recently retired as a Lieutenant Colonel in the Ohio Army National Guard. I started as a young private in the Infantry... and that is a topic for another book.

I also teach a semester long course on Personal Finance at Sinclair Community College across from the Kings Island Amusement Park in Mason, Ohio.

These experiences provide our clients and potential clients solid guidance and advice.

# APPENDIX C:
# FIVE-STAR TESTIMONIALS

★ ★ ★ ★ ★

Four years ago our family's financial situation began to take a turn for the worse which caused our family to fall behind on our mortgage payments. The mortgage company was taking steps to foreclose on our home. I had no idea where to even begin or what I needed to do to save my family's home. I have three children and also take care of my elderly father whom also lives with us; so losing the house was not an option. Not even knowing where to start as far as catching up on the mortgage payments, I started to search for a reputable attorney. That is when Attorney Ryan Ruehle was recommended to me. After going to Ryan's office and meeting with him and discussing a plan of action, I knew that he was the attorney for us. Ryan right away started on our Chapter 13. It has been a rough three years keeping up with the finances, the emergencies that arise when raising three children, the unexpected repairs and upkeep that go along with owning a home, etc. There were several times where we got behind on a few Chapter 13 payments but Ryan was always there going the extra mile helping us through the rough times and getting us past them. Ryan Ruehle in my opinion is one of the best attorneys that I have ever worked with and he is exactly the miracle that my family needed. It is because of him that I was able to keep a roof over my children's heads. Over the course of the past three years that I have been working with Ryan he has always shown nothing but the upmost respect for myself and my family. Ryan takes pride in his work and generally cares for his clients, ultimately not just seeing us as his next paycheck or vacation to the Caribbean but seeing us as actual human beings trying to make a living and provide for my family. I'm sure Ryan has a very heavy work load and cases that are more demanding than our family's Chapter 13, but whenever I interact with Ryan you can tell that he truly cares about you and that he will do everything that is in his power to help. I truly appreciate everything that he has done for myself and for my family. He is one of the best and I would recommend him to anyone. Not only is Ryan an amazing attorney, he is a man of character, a man of integrity and a man who truly cares about each and every one of his clients as an individual that matters. Thank you Ryan, my family and I are so very grateful for everything that you have done for us.

—M.S.

★ ★ ★ ★ ★

Nervous, scared, ashamed and embarrassed was how I felt walking in to Ryan's office the first time I met him. Right away I could tell that Ryan was caring, understanding, compassionate, patient and above all knowledgeable. I was struggling with the emotional aspect side of filing bankruptcy. Ryan

sensed that and was very deliberate in his explanation of the process. His image of "jumping over the line" helped me visualize what I needed to do. May sound silly, but it was what I needed. Did I mention patient? He was extra patient with me, when I had questions, he answered them in a way that made me feel comfortable. From start to finish he made sure that my concerns and fears were addressed. He even managed to get a smile from me at the meeting with the creditors and Trustee. Ryan I can't thank you enough for helping me get life back! Actually, you saved my life from despair and desperation to a place where I have a chance to rebuild and succeed. 5 star in my book!
—C.B.

★★★★★

I am finishing up a 5 year experience of a Chapter 13 filing. The experience has been gut wrenching and heart breaking, as my wife died within 6 months of the filing, creating unimaginable complications to a very difficult process. Throughout, Ryan has been by my side creating answers, as well as comfort, that all can and will work out. Ryan always had an answer for the Trustee and the Court that I would stay the course and get through the case. The case is being discharged this month; thanks so much Ryan for all that you did!!!!!!!!!!!!!
—B.T.

# YOUR NEXT STEPS

Thank you for spending time with me and letting me pull back the curtain on the bankruptcy process and lay to rest some common misconceptions about how it works and what you can expect from it.

In exchange for your investment in time, I'd like to reciprocate and offer you a free gift. I currently charge my bankruptcy clients $295.00 for a 60-minute consultation. But if you call our offices and mention this book, that fee will be entirely waived.

Come in and talk to me. We will dig down together and figure out what's *really* happening with your debt and what strategies you can use to reclaim your future and your freedom.

Please call our offices to schedule this private, completely confidential consultation. It won't cost you a penny, and the benefits for your peace of mind will be priceless. Looking forward to hearing from you shortly,

*Ryan J. Really (Ruehle)*

## Take Action Today Toward
## YOUR NEW FUTURE!

Call our office TODAY!
Make your appointment for a
FREE CONSULTATION
**(A $295.00 value)**

# Find RELIEF
## And Get Back In Control of
## Your Future!

### Call: (513) 621-0999
### www.GETREALLYLEGAL.com

*I will share all of your options.*
*Your Future Awaits!*

www.ingramcontent.com/pod-product-compliance
Lightning Source LLC
Chambersburg PA
CBHW061841220326
41599CB00027B/5363